Thinking of...

Relocating to Silicon Valley?

Ask the Smart Questions

By Natalie Gotts and Ian Gotts

Copyright © 2019 Natalie Gotts and Ian Gotts

First Published in 2019 by Smart Questions Limited, Fryern House, 125 Winchester Road, Chandlers Ford, Hampshire, SO53 2DR, UK
Web: *www.smart-questions.com* (including ordering of printed and electronic copies, extended book information, community contributions and details on charity donations)
Email: *info@smart-questions.com* (for customer services, bulk order enquiries, reproduction requests et al)

The right of Natalie Gotts and Ian Gotts to be identified as the authors of this book has been asserted in accordance with the Copyright, Designs and Patents Act 1998. All rights reserved. No part of this publication may be reproduced, stored in a retrieval system or transmitted, in any form or by any means, electronic, mechanical, recording or otherwise, in any part of the world, without the prior permission of the publisher. Requests for permission should be sent to the publisher at *info@smart-questions.com*

Designations used by entities to distinguish their products are often claimed as trade marks. All brand names and product names used in this book are trade names, service marks, trade marks or registered trademarks of their respective owners.

The authors and publisher have taken care in preparation of this book, but to the extent permitted by applicable laws make no express or implied warranty of any kind and assume no responsibility for errors or omissions. The contents of this book are general in nature and do not constitute legal or other professional advice. You should always seek specific professional advice relevant to your circumstances. Where specific costs or prices have been given, these represent our best 'standard case' estimates at the time of writing. They are intended to provide a rough indication only and should not be relied on in any way. To the extent permitted by law, no liability is assumed for direct, incidental or consequential loss or damage suffered or incurred in connection with or arising out of the use of the information contained herein.

A catalogue record for this book is available from the British Library.

ISBN 978-1-907453-26-7

SQ-23-197-001-001

Smart Questions™ Philosophy

Smart Questions is built on 3 key pillars, which set it apart from other publishers:

1. *Smart people want Smart Questions not Dumb Answers*
2. *Domain experts are often excluded from authorship, so we are making writing a book simple and painless*
3. *The community has a great deal to contribute to enhance the content*

www.smart-questions.com

Authors

Natalie Gotts

Lead singer and manager of a rock band, Jane Blonde and the Goldfingers, Natalie has managed 3 transatlantic family moves singlehandedly. So, she has first-hand knowledge of what it takes to make the transition as smooth, stress free and cost effective for everyone involved.

She is also extremely good at planning vacations and seems to be able to sniff out the perfect hotel, the entertaining tour guide and the best expeditions.

Email: natalie.gotts@gmail.com

Ian Gotts

A serial tech entrepreneur and advisor where his passion and

energy are infectious and inspiring. He was founder and CEO of NimbusPartners, which was bought by TIBCO Software. He is CEO and founder of Elements.cloud an app that helps clean-up, document and drive adoption of Salesforce. He is an author of 11 books with a rare ability to make the complex seem simple which makes him a sought after and entertaining conference speaker.

And he is powered by Duracell.

Email: ian.gotts@gmail.com

 Blog for the book: *http://movetosv.wordpress.com*

Table of Contents

1 Digital gold rush is here in SV 1

2 You need to be here 3

3 Go big or go home 7

4 The US is the graveyard for UK companies 11

5 Life changing 15

6 Ask the Smart Questions 17

7 The known unknowns 21

8 Moving Your Life: BC 25

9 Moving Your Life: AC 57

10 Other considerations 77

11 It wasn't like that for me 87

12 The Final Word 95

Who should read this book?

People like you and me

This book has been written for anyone who is relocating to Silicon Valley from mainland Europe, South Africa, Australia and New Zealand. It has been written based on our UK experience, but distance of these other countries from the West Coast makes the logistics challenges similar.

You could be an employee being seconded to the US or an entrepreneur or executive looking to drive US growth. This is not aimed at refugees or asylum seekers!!

This book is intended to be a catalyst for action aimed both at the person moving and their partner, who will probably pick up much of the logistics planning and execution.

The person moving

This is both exciting and scary. A step into the unknown. So, you need to focus on the job at hand – your new assignment in the US.

Therefore, this book aims to remove the stress of the move by giving you the lists of what you need to do.

The spouse/partner of the person moving

Through the book we call this person the Supporter.

The Supporter is probably going the bear the brunt of the moving logistics, which is not insignificant especially if you have children and pets to move as well. The move is likely to cause more stress across the family than anything so far in your relationship.

This book will help you ask the Smart Questions, because if you don't it may put your relationship at risk.

How to use this book

This book is intended to be the catalyst for action. We hope that the ideas and examples presented in this book will inspire you to act. So, do whatever you need to do to make this book useful. Use Post-it notes, write on it, rip it apart, or read it quickly in one sitting. Whatever works for you. We hope this becomes your most dog-eared book.

Chapter 1

Digital gold rush is here in SV

Gold! Gold! Gold from the American River!

San Francisco newspaper publisher and merchant Samuel Brannan strode through the streets of San Francisco, holding aloft a vial of gold in 1848

EVERYONE wants to be a Silicon Valley rock star. And they can. It has never been easier to develop a tech solution and get it to the market; powerful development platforms, hosting partners, app exchanges and funding. At the same time, there has been the rise of the celebrity tech entrepreneur fuelled by films like "The Social Network" and "Jobs" and the TV program "Silicon Valley".

This has driven what feels like a digital gold rush, reminiscent of the 1849 Gold Rush. Silicon Valley is "the" destination for pioneers intent on working in a tech business. Sure, you could be in Houston, New York, London or Tel Aviv. But Silicon Valley is where the tech heart beats strongest.

It has an unrivalled pool of successful entrepreneurs, funding and tech-savvy employees. The depth and strength of these can't be easily replicated anywhere else in the world. It's a virtuous spiral creating what feels like a self-fulfilling prophecy.

And by Silicon Valley we include the city of San Francisco and its suburbs. And if you have any serious aspirations to grow a significant size global company, then you need to plan to launch here sometime soon.

However, moving you and family half way across the world is a major commitment. It takes time, planning and a lot of money. That investment should payback 10x or 100x but it does require a committed and focused approach.

When planning and executing the move, no one decision kills you, but it's death by a 1000 cuts. There are so many little decisions and actions that if got wrong, are not insurmountable but waste time or money. And both time and money are the most precious resource.

Chapter 2

You need to be here

Weather wonderful. Wish you were here.
British postcard

WE spent 15 years building an enterprise software company to a reasonable size with blue chip clients across the world. But it wasn't until we moved the CEO and COO to San Francisco that things started to accelerate. Within 7 months we had an offer of huge levels of investment and an offer to buy the business. We took the exit as it was the right answer for the clients, employees and shareholders.

Now we live in San Francisco where we have become avid students of "the Silicon Valley way". Not that it's set in stone, as it's constantly changing and morphing. For example, Silicon Valley now includes the City of San Francisco, which has become a hotbed for tech start-ups and incubators. So much so that the VCs are moving out of Sand Hill Road and opening offices in the City.

But we have been struck by how different the experiences are between the UK and Silicon Valley.

These comments are empirical and not backed up with hard data. So, it's gut feel. But many recognize that the most valuable but under-used resource for senior executives is being able to listen to their gut or intuition.

Size of market

Clearly the USA has significantly more consumers and corporate buyers than the UK. In fact, the population of the US is 320 million, nearly 5 times that of the UK and the idea of the "United States of Europe" is a non-starter due to the cultural, language and economic differences between the countries. Having 320m consumers on your doorstep, all speaking the same business language and having broadly the same attitude makes all the difference. It means you can support the entire country with one (or max two) languages, one data centre, one legal entity, one set of contracts… and the list goes on.

In fact, it colours every other factor, which we have considered.

Let me give you some numbers to chew on, which illustrate the size of the market.

A software platform for yoga studios? For beauty shops? Tour guides? These are small businesses with small budgets. How could there possibly be enough demand?

A company providing booking software for yoga studios, which is valued at more than $450 million, has over 500,000 practitioners who use its platform and annual revenue run rate of around $50 million. It taps into a (very large) niche market, but one where every participant has the same problem.

Attitude

In the USA there is no such thing as failure, only feedback. To create something really special means taking risk. And risk means you sometimes fail. That is acceptable in the USA. But also, it's good to succeed. There is no UK "tall poppy syndrome here", nor the stigma of failing. That breeds a very different type of entrepreneur. One that is positive, risk taking and celebrates success.

Funding

Take a huge market and bet on a management team to make it big. That is the approach for funding in the US. Not that the money is given away without some thought, but it's true venture capital. It's risk capital. The UK funding environment seems as risk averse as a bank, and the small UK market means the bets are small. As the potential US market is large, then VCs understand that once a level of product traction is gained, then substantial levels of funding are required to scale. But the first priority is not necessarily a clear business model or profitability.

Which leads me to my next point. The greatest criticism we hear from UK entrepreneurs, is that the US funding approach is not realistic; that companies with no proven business model or idea of how they're going to become profitable, are funded. They say that this is not a credible approach. But then you look at the number of companies that have scaled up and then become wildly valuable and profitable or acquired before they reached profitability. Companies in both B2C and B2B that include LinkedIn, Twitter, Facebook, PayPal, YouTube, Salesforce, Groupon, Eloqua, Exact Target, Yammer, Airbnb and the list goes on and on. But the approach is made possible by a combination of the market size, the attitudes and the funding appetite.

Serial entrepreneurs are everywhere

With some many entrepreneurs, there are a huge number of people who have been very successful, many of who never need work again. But they do. They achieve success after success. Perhaps because they're financially secure they're prepared to take greater risks. But also, because they have proven they can do it, VCs are falling over themselves to fund them. So, the entrepreneurs don't even need to use their own money. And with every company they're teaching, coaching and mentoring their employees to be entrepreneurs, And, finally they become investors either as individuals, syndicates or VCs.

At a corporate event in Las Vegas, I interviewed Tom Siebel, founder of Siebel Systems, for a video case study. He sold Siebel Systems to Oracle and according to Wikipedia he is worth $1.8bn. But when we met, he was all fired up about his latest venture *C3Energy.com* At the same event I met Scott McNealy, co-founder of Sun Microsystems, which when it was sold to Oracle must have made Scott a billionaire. But he was manning the exhibition stand with his brother pitching his latest venture, not out on the golf course.

Support and coaching

In the UK, as success and riches are in short supply, people seem unwilling to give support and advice for free. They want a little piece of the action. This desire to get something for everything has been termed "Mr 1%". Out here, advice is freely given with no expectation of some payback. What goes around comes around seems to be the approach – a form of tech karma. However, not everything is a free ride. When you need solid advice there is a strong ecosystem of advisory firms who know how to bill you!!

Education and networking

Again, with so many successful entrepreneurs, there is a willingness to share their knowledge and experience. So, VCs, lawyers and advisors are constantly running events to showcase their clients and get entrepreneurs together. It's great education and networking for entrepreneurs, but also good business for the hosts who get to spot the rising stars.

Weather

Finally, it's sunny here for a great deal of the year. It may sound stupid, but when you're waking up to clear skies and lunching outside, then everyone has a happier and more positive attitude. If you spend your weekends outside, then you're healthier and return to work on Monday invigorated and recharged. And that leads to higher productivity and business optimism. How different is that attitude when you're subjected to grey and cold for over six months of the year?

There are clear links between happy people and productivity, which we highlighted in a blog called Happy staff? I run a business, not a holiday camp.

British accent

Add in the fact that your British accent credits you with an extra 15 IQ points and Californian sunshine makes everyone feel good, and you've got a bubble of positivity. What more can you need to grow a business and career?

Chapter 3

Go big or go home

It's a lot easier just to write big checks than it is to innovate

Marc Benioff (Chairman & CEO, salesforce.com, 1964 -)

Decide on the level of commitment. You don't necessarily need to up sticks and emigrate with your entire family to the US. You could come for a 2-year period. You could commute 2 weeks a month for 5 years — mad but entirely possible. There are various levels of commitment. But you do need to agree up front where you — as individuals and your family who are coming to the US - sit on the spectrum, because it will affect every other decision.

The spectrum is below.

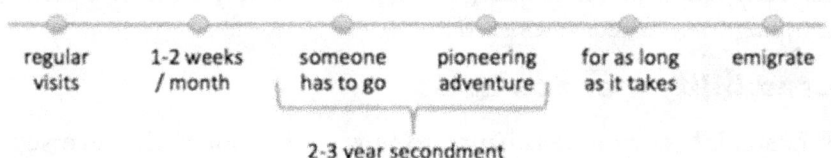

Big market, big investment, big ambition.

In the previous chapter we made a pretty good case for the US in terms of size of market and size of opportunity. But what that means is if you come to the US you need to play by US rules. If you bring a British risk averse, conservative attitude you will simply not be taken seriously. In simple terms - "Go big or go home."

Sometimes is seems incredible that companies are able to raise – and spend – such huge sums of money. You may not be responsible for corporate strategy, but it is useful to understand the thinking. Funding broadly goes into 3 areas; sales and marketing, people and infrastructure.

Growth is important. Profit can come later.

For many early-stage companies - i.e. less than 5 years old – their focus is on growth and momentum. Top line revenue growth is an important, or possibly the only, metric. Profit is less of an issue as the aim to expand the market penetration, grow customers and resulting revenue. Dialling back on sales and marketing spend to make a profit compromises that growth. Plus, investors want to see their capital being put to work. They want to see it being spent and turned into revenue growth, so they can invest more.

Big country = big flights = big burn rate

The high levels spend on sales people and expenses are because the US is a huge country. Any sales call or marketing event in another city requires a flight and overnight stay and internal flights and hotels are not cheap. The alternatively is to build sales teams in each of the major cities in the US where you have a market. Don't be fooled into thinking that you can build a product, throw up a webpage and watch the customers arrive. There are too many well-funded and marketed products and solutions for you to be heard above the noise, unless you're making some noise of your own. So, the company will be spending money - big money – on a marketing campaign and direct sales staff.

Credibility – execs in US

Whilst a UK corporate is happy to buy a US product, the reverse is not true. American's are very patriotic and like to buy from a US company. If this is not a US company, then is must be US subsidiary of a UK company that is fully – 110% - committed to the US. That means your US organization needs to be headed by one of the executive team – preferably one of the founders.

We were staggered by the change in attitude and results when we relocated some of the executive team to the US. Whilst I was CEO of Nimbus, we grew the US operation to 15 people – sales consultants and support – with a very credible ex-Accenture US national leading the team. We were able to win pilots and small follow-on projects, but we were never able to close the enterprise deal with our US clients. Until I moved out to San Francisco with my COO and Head of Training. It was like a light had been switched on. Suddenly we were being taken seriously by major US corporates and deals started flowing. Sad but true.

The US clients simply wanted to be sure that we were committed to selling and supporting the US market before they made a strategic software purchase. Completely understandable if you look at it from their position. And you may argue that you can sell to and support the US from the UK by working US hours and changing the spelling on your website. You think you can give the impression that you're really in the US, it doesn't work. Lots of things give it away. The office hours are not the same, the public holidays and hence the office closures are not the same, the accents of the staff on the support desks are not American, and the centre of gravity of the company is not in the US. To support the US, you really need to be in the US. Either do or don't do it. Doing it half-heartedly means you will never get the true value for the investment you make in the US.

Go big or go home

Chapter 4

The US is the graveyard for UK companies

My sense is that what they tried to do was make a European model

Prof Anthony Dukes, USC Marshall School of Business, on Tesco's closure of 199 Fresh & Easy West Coast stores costing £1.2bn

MOST UK companies see the US as an important market but are frightened off by the horror stories from company after company who have tried and failed to make their mark on the US. There are so many ways to get it wrong and all end up with the huge losses and an embarrassing retrenchment back to the home market.

Most companies don't appreciate the investment, focus and effort it takes to build a credible US operation. There is a good reason why US companies raise SO much investment. It gets spent on staff, travel expenses, offices, servers and marketing. Without that financial support you're bringing a knife to a gunfight.

But it's not just a lack of investment that can kill you. Let's start to look at the different ways it can go pear-shaped:

Bringing a UK attitude

You have been successful in the UK with an approach that possibly goes like this: organic growth, low risk, minimize cash burn, get profitable in 1st 6 months. To an American's eyes that approach lacks ambition. It's way too conservative. Our mantra (eventually) was, "go big or go home". This was when we moved the CEO, COO and Head of Training to the US. However, this was 7 years after we had hired our first US employee. The intervening 7 years were lack lustre and it took all that time to have enough balls and funding to be able to do it properly. But more of that later. You need to play the American's at their own game. US company after company has lost money for 10+ years – LinkedIn, YouTube, Amazon, Salesforce, Google, PayPal, Box, and the list goes on and on. They focus on revenue growth. They become a market leader and either dominate their sector, which suddenly allows them to become profitable, or they're acquired for a multiple of revenue, not profit.

Look and act like US company

You need to make it easy for US customers to buy your product or service. That means looking like a US company. Acting like a US company. Operating like a US company.

That has implications across the board. US website with US spelling. US marketing materials with US sized paper. US support desk with US accents. US invoicing and a US bank account.

Loud and proud. The staff and company have LinkedIn profiles, entries on Crunchbase.com and reviews on GlassDoor.com. But you don't need to lose elements of your Britishness. A British accent is worth an extra 15 IQ points. So, lose the British inhibitions and big yourself up. Understatement is lost here.

Hitchhikers Guide to the Galaxy - Douglas Adams

An example of the quintessential British understatement comes from HHG. Arthur Dent (Brit) and Zaphod Beeblebrox (from a planet in the vicinity of Betelgeuse) and Trillian (human) are about to be destroyed by Magrathea's guided missiles.

> TRILLIAN: It's no good the missiles are swinging round after us and gaining fast. We are quite definitely going to die.
>
> ARTHUR: Why doesn't anyone turn on this Improbability Drive thing?
>
> TRILLIAN: Oh, don't be silly you can't do that!
>
> ARTHUR: Why not? There's nothing to lose at this stage.
>
> TRILLIAN: Well because… does anyone know why Arthur can't turn on the Improbability Drive?

The US is the graveyard for UK companies

> TRILLIAN: I said does anyone know --?
>
> [There is a loud explosion, then soft music begins...]
>
> ZAPHOD: Er, what the hell happened?
>
> ARTHUR: Well I was just saying, there's this switch here you see, and if I -
>
> ZAPHOD: Where are we Trillian?
>
> TRILLIAN: Exactly where we were, I think.
>
> ZAPHOD: Then what's happened to the missiles?
>
> FORD: Well, er, according to this screen they've just turned into a bowl of petunias and a very surprised-looking whale.
>
> EDDIE the onboard computer: At an improbability factor of eight million, seven-hundred-and-sixty-seven-thousand, one-hundred-and-twenty-eight to one against.
>
> ZAPHOD: Did you think of that Earthman?
>
> ARTHUR: Well, I did, it was just -
>
> ZAPHOD: That's very good thinking, you know that? You've just saved our lives.
>
> ARTHUR: It was nothing really...
>
> ZAPHOD: Oh, was it? Oh, well forget it.

Commitment

As we said earlier, you need to throw yourself into it. It's not a vacation or a short-term secondment. You need to assume you're in for the long haul. You need to set expectations with your family. Nothing kills your ability to be effective more than an unhappy family pining to go back home. The best attitude is to treat it as a fantastic adventure and make the most of the trip. Don't put your life on hold whilst in the US, waiting to return to the UK.

You need to make sure that you have estimated the costs so you can maintain the same standard of living here. It's expensive to live in the Bay area; houses, cleaners, babysitters, food, eating out, sports clubs... And there is limited public transport outside the city, so expect to use cars a lot. But at least petrol is cheap.

Don't run out of cash. You need to budget for at least 2 years, as it will take that long to establish the company as a local company and here to stay. Ideally you need to be planning for longer.

But it's not all negative. The Bay area is a fantastic place to live. The business opportunities. The vibrant outdoor lifestyle. The chance to explore another area of the world that is now within reach.

Someone once said "Life is like a sewer. The more you put into it, the more you get out of it."

Devil is in the detail

Moving is a 3-6 month project with a number of key dependencies which require meticulous planning. And some things are far easier done from the UK than when you get to the US. No one item will kill you, but every mistake you make will cost you time and money. Both of which are in short supply.

Which is the point of this book. To help you think of all the things that need to be decided, planned and executed.

Chapter 5

Life changing

When you do what you fear most, then you can do anything
Stephen Richards (author of The Cosmic Ordering Guide)

IF there's one thing we've learnt from our three trans-Atlantic moves, it's that they're life changing.

Firstly, our parents didn't take too kindly to the idea of their loved ones moving 6,000 miles away. Regular Skype calls are no substitute. They needed reassurance, compassion and invitations for long visits. The home we chose needed to be able to accommodate them.

Secondly, our children needed support through the process. Our son threw a 10-month-long hissy fit before, during and after the first move. He still refers to the UK as home, several years later. Our daughter, who was determined to be excited by the idea, wanted reassurance in the form of the repetition of exact details of what was going to happen on every single day of the preparation. You know your children best, but you may be surprised by their reactions.

Thirdly, moving to America is like an earthquake – which is probably too poignant a simile given that we moved to California. The shaking of the earth topples weak buildings and only the strongest structures survive. The same applied to the structures in our lives; friendships, hobbies, employment, and homes were all questioned and many of them didn't survive the earthquake.

But that seismic shift brought huge opportunities with it. We discovered that friends who were friends only through habit weren't a great loss, but those that persevered despite a 6,000 distance are priceless. Hobbies that were continued by rote had lost their appeal anyway. New employment meant new experiences and skills learnt. A new home was a breath of fresh air.

But there was more. Moving everything we owned into a 40' container provided an opportunity to clear out unwanted clutter. We decimated our wardrobes and toy chests. We donated the contents of the cellar to the family, charities or sold it on eBay.

We've made new friends in America surprisingly quickly and are inspired by their varied experiences. We've found new hobbies in California that are made possible by the climate. We've acquired new skills, and we're living in a home where we seem to live outside as much as inside.

Most importantly, each trans-Atlantic move has made us appreciate what we are leaving. Before leaving Britain, we wrote a Bucket List of places we wanted to see that we wouldn't necessarily come back for. We'd return for Christmas and family events, but on those occasions, we wouldn't have time to see, for example, summer solstice at Stonehenge. It's a fact of expat life that each time you return to your home country, your time is filled with visits to family and friends and there's no opportunity for sightseeing.

So, what's on your Bucket List?

Chapter 6

Ask the Smart Questions

If I have seen further, it is by standing on the shoulders of giants
Isaac Newton (Scientist, 1643 – 1727)

SMART Questions is about giving you valuable insights or "the Smarts". Normally these are only gained through years of painful and costly experience. Whether you already have a general understanding of the subject and need to take it to the next level or are starting from scratch, you need to make sure you ask the Smart Questions. We aim to short circuit that learning process, by providing the expertise of the 'giants' that Isaac Newton referred to.

Not all the questions will necessarily be new or staggeringly insightful. The value you get from the information will clearly vary. It depends on your job role and previous experience. We call this the 3Rs.

The 3 Rs

Some of the questions will be in areas where you know the answers already so the book will **Reinforce** them in your mind.

You may have forgotten some aspects of the subject, so the book will **Remind** you.

Other questions may **Reveal** new insights to you that you've never considered before.

How do you use Smart Questions?

The structure of the questions is set out in Chapter 7, and the questions are in Chapters 8, 9 and 10. The questions are laid out in a series of structured and ordered tables with the questions in one column and the explanation of why it matters alongside. We've also provided a checkbox so that you can mark which questions are relevant to your particular situation.

A quick scan down the first column in the list of questions should give you a general feel of where you are for each question vs. the 3Rs.

At the highest level they are a sanity check or checklist of areas to consider. Just one question may save you a whole heap of cash or heartache.

At the end we've tried to bring some of the questions to life with some stories of people who have made the move.

We trust that you will find real insights. There may be some 'aha' moments. Hopefully not too many sickening, 'head in the hands – what have we done' moments.

In this context, probably the most critical role of the questions is that they reveal risks that you hadn't considered. On the flip side they should also open up your thinking to opportunities that you hadn't necessarily considered.

How to dig deeper

Need more information? Not convinced by the examples, or want ones that are more relevant to your specific situation? You can contact the authors (their email addresses have been provided in the "Authors" section at the beginning of the book).

And finally

Please remember that these questions are NOT intended to be a prescriptive list that must be followed slavishly from beginning to end. It's also inevitable that the list of questions is not exhaustive, and we are confident that with the help of the community the list of Smart Questions will grow.

Ask the Smart Questions

If you want to rephrase a question to improve its context or have identified a question we've missed, then let us know to add to the collective knowledge.

We also understand that not all of the questions will apply to all people. However, we encourage you to read them all, as there may be a nugget of truth that can be adapted to your circumstances.

Above all we do hope that it provides a guide or a pointer to the areas that may be valuable to you and helps with the "3 Rs".

Ask the Smart Questions

The known unknowns

There are known knowns. These are things we know that we know. There are known unknowns. That is to say, there are things that we now know we don't know. But there are also unknown unknowns. These are things we don't know we don't know.

Donald Rumsfeld (former US Defense Secretary, 1932 -)

OPPORTUNITY and risk are two sides of the same coin. There is no real opportunity without risk. Every businessperson knows that, but not everyone embraces the two essential risks to every opportunity – decision and change. First, you need to decide on a direction; then you need to make adjustments and innovations to keep going and growing.

There are clear benefits to moving to the US, but they're not necessarily worth the risk for every business or individual. The questions in the next chapters help you consider every aspect of the opportunity to be able to estimate the risks effectively.

Clearly not all the questions will be a surprise to you, but there are some areas, particularly in the Moving your life chapters (which are all about the logistics of the move), that may not have occurred to you. They certainly didn't to us the first time around, and they caught us out.

Which is why this book is so valuable. You're learning from our successes and mistakes.

The known unknowns

To help you through this transition, the questions have been grouped into the following structure:

Chapter 8: Moving your life: BC

1. Timing
2. Look-see visit
3. What should you do with your house?
4. What about US accommodation?
5. Cars
6. Kids and education
7. How to survive 2 months in "limbo"
8. Pets
9. What does your Supporting do?
10. Finance
11. What gets shipped in the container?

Chapter 9: Moving your life: AC

1. Packing the container
2. Cars
3. Getting rid of "stuff" you're not taking; donate, dump or drink?
4. Medical, dental, optical
5. Cancelling stuff and new addresses
6. Leaving parties
7. Flying to the US and arriving in one piece: a long, emotional day
8. Unpacking the container

Chapter 10: Other considerations

1. Why bother?
2. Is there enough budget allocated?
3. Visas
4. Fitting into the US culture

Some terminology

Earner – the person who is driving the move to the US

Supporter – the spouse/partner, who is moving with the Earner to the US

Silicon Valley, the Bay Area, San Francisco. These are all used interchangeably when viewing them from the UK. Once you get here you will understand the differences, but for planning purposes before you arrive, they're the same.

BC and AC. Moving your life has 2 distinct phases:

- **BC – Before the container**. Before the container is packed onto a truck to the port, there are a slew of things that need to be decided and organized. Some of them can be delayed until after the container has left: AC.
- **AC - After the container**. Once the container has gone, you're committed, but there are still things to be done before you get on the plane to start your new adventure.

It's really important to understand that once your container has been packed, you've left – even if you're still in your home country. Most people think (and we made the mistake the first time too) that you don't leave the country until you get on a plane, but that's not the case at all. Once the container leaves, you're also committed to leaving. You probably won't have access to 99% of your belongings for your remaining time in Britain and, wherever you stay after that point, you'll feel as if you're camping or on holiday. You'll possibly feel a little homeless. And a lot excited.

Even if a catastrophe occurred, or you just got really cold feet, your container is going to be on the water for two months to America and another two months back.

The departure of the container is Big.

The known unknowns

Chapter 8

Moving Your Life: BC

Every day is a new day, and you'll never be able to find happiness if you don't move on

Carrie Underwood (American musician)

THIS is a transformational adventure. You're moving your life and family 6,000 miles away. When you get here and start filling in forms, you quite often tick a box marked "alien". And in many ways, it does feel like you're an alien. Things feel familiar because you have seen them in films, but don't let that fool you. Five years on, we're still surprised by things that we don't understand, simply because they're slightly different. Not wrong. Just different.

There may be a small number of you who haven't collected a houseful of belongings (clothes, furniture, toys), don't have kids and don't have pets. If that's the case, you probably don't need a container. You can just get on a plane with a few bags of luggage. However, there are questions in these chapters that are still very relevant to you.

8.1 Timing – when should you move?

There are a number of factors. Some you have control over, and some you don't.

You can't control the time that it takes to get your visa. Once you have a visa, then you have more control. But you don't determine when school terms start and end. Or the availability of the "perfect" house.

You might want to consider staggering your move. The Earner could long-distance-commute before the Supporter and family arrive. It's not ideal, but it's achievable.

Whatever date you choose will ultimately be a compromise. You just need to make sure that you have considered all the issues and understood their impact and relative importance.

Moving Your Life: BC > Timing – when should you move?

☒	Question	Why this matters
☐	8.1.1 Move all at the same time?	Can/should the Earner move at a different time from the Supporter and family? The Supporter never moves first. The timing for the Earner's move is possibly different from the timing for the rest of the family.
☐	8.1.2 Is school driving the timing?	Are you going to wait until the end of a term – bearing in mind the terms aren't the same in the US? Or perhaps the end of the school year? Are you changing of school type (e.g. middle to high school).
☐	8.1.3 Does the Supporter have commitments?	Are there constraints due to the Supporters work or other commitments?
☐	8.1.4 Are there Tax year implications?	You need to consider how many days in UK vs. USA for tax reasons. If you arrive before Jan 1^{st,} then you incur tax liabilities (and cost of completing tax return) for whole year - California double taxation…
☐	8.1.5 Have you completed the Bucket list?	Is there "unfinished business" in the UK?
☐	8.1.6 Are there family commitments?	Christmas, weddings, get-togethers, graduations (e.g. getting everyone in same country for "goodbye")
☐	8.1.7 Other commitments?	What else have you committed to? Hobbies: finish the sailing season, playing for a team, performances, courses, parties?
☐	8.1.8 How much help is required?	The Earner's job is dictating the move, therefore he/she is working and not helping with the move. Don't underestimate how much time it takes for the supporter. It's very labour intensive.
☐	8.1.9 Extended family's needs?	Will parents/grandparents want you to stay in your home country for as long as possible?

Moving Your Life: BC > Timing – when should you move?

☒	Question	Why this matters
☐	8.1.10 Are you coming back?	If you're going for, say, two years or more, does the return time affect your departure time? Moving back isn't just "moving back home" but finding new social groups / schools / house / cars. It's as big a move as moving out to US.

8.2 Look see visit

This may be the first time the Supporter and the rest of the family have ever visited San Francisco and the Bay Area, so the trip is part investigation and part sales job. It needs to be fun as well as effective. Fortunately, San Francisco is a fantastic location (the number of tourists here prove that it's a holiday bucket list city). Factor in enough time to make it feel like a vacation.

This is not the right place to be providing sightseeing advice. But we have crowd-sourced from San Francisco locals a wealth of "inside knowledge". You can find it in our free eBook.

Getting around SF and the Bay Area: did you know the Richmond Bridge ONLY takes cash?

The coolest boutique hotels: avoiding the standard Hiltons and Hyatts.

Where the locals eat: locals' favourite haunts.

Being a tourist: there's the obvious stuff, but there other really cool things to do that aren't in the guidebooks.

Venturing further afield: Route 1, the Wine Country, Yosemite and whale watching.

With kids: if the children are happy, parents are happy too.

You can download the eBook here: *http://bit.ly/gottsSF*

☒	Question	Why this matters
☐	8.2.1 What is the objective?	What do you want to achieve? Convince Supporter it's worth moving? Find the perfect office and house location? Look at schools? Validate costs of living? All of the above?
☐	8.2.2 Multiple trips and for how long?	You may need to go once to get a feel for the place and again once you have visas. It's easy to get around the Bay area, but don't underestimate the time it takes to look at houses, schools, offices and add in touristy bits.
☐	8.2.3 When is the best time to do look see?	If you're looking at rental houses, you don't want to look-see more than 3 months in advance. If your look-see visit will determine whether or not you move, you might want to consider reconnaissance up to a year in advance. You may need multiple trips but could combine them with work.
☐	8.2.4 When should you tell the children?	You know your children's characters best. Do they deal well with change? Do they like adventure? Are they old enough to cope with uncertainty? Do you want to involve them in the discussion or present the move as a *fait accompli*? Will they be reassured if they can help with choosing somewhere to live? How much warning before school visits do you think they need to adjust to the idea?
☐	8.2.5 When should you visit prospective schools?	Chapter 8.6 is devoted to schools. Public (state) schools in your chosen area are obliged to provide space for your children. Private schools will probably want your children to spend a day at the school to see if they're a good fit.
☐	8.2.6 Is it too soon to look at rental properties?	You can use the trip to meet realtors, check location, how's the commute, what's the budget, what's the weather (fog)?

Moving Your Life: BC > Look see visit

☒	Question	Why this matters
☐	8.2.7 Are there any deal-breakers?	Could anything come up that would cause you to reconsider your move? Can't find decent school / house / neighbourhood / weather? Do you need to identify your deal-breakers in advance, or do you have to find a way to work around them?
☐	8.2.8 Are you looking at office locations?	Think about commute times, parking costs vs. public transport. The ferry is an idyllic commute but not cheap.
☐	8.2.9 Realistic agenda?	It should be a balance of work and play, client and move planning. Have you planned to do too much especially if you're all dealing with jet-lag?
☐	8.2.10 What evaluation measures will you use?	How to you evaluate the visit so you can objectively make decisions when back in the UK.

8.3 What should you do with your house?

If you own your house in the UK, what do you do with it? A lot depends on your commitment level. How long are you intending to stay in America, and what are the potential options at the end of your secondment?

It's impossible to predict the future. There are so many unanswerable questions, such as: Are you coming back to the same house in the UK? Will you sell your company and be able to come back and buy that dream house? Could you end up staying in San Francisco for longer than you anticipate?

It's great to have big dreams about the future, but it's probably best to make decisions about your home in Britain with the information you have in front of you: i.e. a secondment contract and a 3-year visa.

Moving Your Life: BC > What should you do with your house?

☒	Question	Why this matters
☐	8.3.1 Should you sell or let your house?	How long moving for? Had look-see trip yet? Need a pad to come back to? How frequent are you visits back and where will you be? Need capital money for move / rental deposit /other? Good rental market for your house?
☐	8.3.2 What should you do with furniture?	If you're letting you house, are you letting it furnished or unfurnished? If renting in the US, are you renting furnished or unfurnished? Who's paying for a container to transport all goods? Who is paying for storage if you decide to store furniture?
☐	8.3.3 If letting UK house, how will you manage the let?	Management agency or proxy friend/family? How will you manage the maintenance? What length of contract should you go for? Who finds new tenants if the existing ones leave or you need to get rid of them? What happens if you come back early?
☐	8.3.4 Ready for renting?	Is your house set up for renting? What last minute DIY jobs need doing – it's way easier to fix now, rather than 6,000 miles away? Where are the instruction manuals for central heating, white goods, alarms? Get an assessment from a rental agent in time for you to make any changes whilst you're in the UK.
☐	8.3.5 Maintenance contacts	Do you have tradesmen who you trust who can fix any problems? The agency will have people, but at premium rates.
☐	8.3.6 From when should you let it?	Want to see it started before moving to the US? But that costs money for you to stay elsewhere.

Moving Your Life: BC > What should you do with your house?

☒	Question	Why this matters
☐	8.3.7 Where do you live while you're between countries?	Once the container is packed, you've left UK. Once it arrives in US, you've arrived. Between those times, whichever country you're in, you're in no-man's land because you don't have your stuff. See whole section on "How to survive Limbo", Chapter 9.7
☐	8.3.8 Tax issues	If you rent the house will you have tax liabilities in both the UK and US.
☐	8.3.9 Break clauses	What happens if you want to come back early? What happens if you want to get rid of the tenants?
☐	8.3.10 Returning	What happens if you return but the house is not available – who pays your rent?
☐	8.3.11 Important documents	Critical documents need to be scanned and originals carried out in hand luggage in case your baggage or container are lost? What documents are required in the 2-month limbo period. e.g. leases, proof of insurance, warranties etc?

8.4 What about US accommodation?

San Francisco is a brutally expensive place to live. The only things we've found that are cheaper than the UK are cinema tickets and yoga classes. Everything else – accommodation, food, schools, services – costs more. If you want to live in the manner to which you've become accustomed in Britain, you need to budget correctly.

And, as in every city, the price of rental property does vary. The farther you're prepared to commute, the cheaper the property.

Then again, this is possibly a rare chance to live in one of the most spectacular areas in the developed world. The Bay, walking in the headlands, biking and sailing are all on your doorstep; wine country is less than an hour away; skiing in Lake Tahoe is less than 4 hours away. You may think it's worth making the most of the area by supplementing your budget for the period of your secondment.

Or maybe you'll decide to compromise on the property and use your budget to travel more widely. San Francisco is a great starting point to explore Hawaii, western US or even Asia.

Would you like to experiment with a change of scene and pace? Swap the English village cottage for a city loft apartment?

If you're buying a property in America, then you need to know that the amount of annual property tax here is not the same as the UK's council tax (a mere £500-£2,000 per year). In America, annual property tax is approximately 1.5% of the purchase price of the property. This means that on a house valued at $1m, the property tax could be $15,000. Every year. And $1m doesn't buy you a very big apartment or house. It's also hard to get a mortgage in your first year here, so you may have to buy a house with cash.

Moving Your Life: BC > What about US accommodation?

☒	Question	Why this matters
☐	8.4.1 Should you rent or buy in US?	How long are you in the US for? Are you able to buy house without mortgage? Aliens can't get mortgage in the US for their first year. Have you factored in the running costs such as insurance and annual property tax?
☐	8.4.2 Rent then buy	Perhaps you should rent for 6 months to get an understanding of the area before you buy?
☐	8.4.3 Priorities vs. budget	What is important: space, commute, schools, views, access to SFO or outdoors?
☐	8.4.4 What's your contract length?	What are the break clauses in case you leave US early? Perhaps you want to have multiple 6-month rentals to explore different areas. This is more achievable if you travel light.
☐	8.4.5 Are you liable if you leave US early?	Breach of contract costs money. Check contract or change it.
☐	8.4.6 How big a house in the US do you need?	When the family visits you they rarely come for just two days. For those with retired parents, they could come for 2 months to escape the winter. How much space do you need?
☐	8.4.7 Who is renting the property?	As an individual you probably haven't got credit rating. So, the company will need to rent on your behalf.
☐	8.4.8 Tax liabilities	What are the tax liabilities for the Earner as the rental will be a taxable benefit? Does the company cover this additional tax?
☐	8.4.9 Allowance	What is the allowance for renting and what happens if the Earner wants to spend less or more?
☐	8.4.10 Location	Space, view, commute, schools, sports, space, community, airport.
☐	8.4.11 Office and home	Are you using the house as a home office, at least initially?

☒	Question	Why this matters
☐	8.4.12 Time to SFO?	SFO is an easy airport to get to, but the traffic patterns vary based on time of the day.

Moving Your Life: BC > Cars

8.5 Cars

Chapter 9 contains the questions that help steer your approach to the cars you own in Britain. This chapter covers your car strategy in America.

The cities of San Francisco and Berkeley are well served by public transport. Silicon Valley and Marin are not. In San Francisco and Berkeley, you might be able to get away with using public transport and the occasional ZipCar (hourly car rental). If you don't have a car in Silicon Valley or Marin, you're stranded.

Buying a car isn't straightforward. To buy a car:

- you need to pay cash (you will have no credit rating)
- you need to have insurance
- which requires you have a US license
- but getting a license means passing the behind-the-wheel test
- which means that you must pass your written theory test and there is often a long (45+ day) wait for the behind-the-wheel test after passing the written test
- to take the written test you need a Social Security Number.

To get access to ZipCar, you need your UK driving record, which can be obtained from DVLA. It's much easier to get this while you're in the UK than it is once you've moved to the US.

Moving Your Life: BC > Cars

☒	Question	Why this matters
☐	8.5.1 Do you REALLY need a car?	If you have no kids and live in the City, owning a car may not be critical. Rental cars, ZipCar, bikes and public transport may be a far cheaper option.
☐	8.5.2 Shipping cars?	Check Californian restrictions. The emissions laws plus all the other modifications make importing very difficult and expensive.
☐	8.5.3 When can you buy?	To buy a car required you have insurance, which requires you have a US license, which takes several months to get. So, you will be renting initially.
☐	8.5.4 Early return	If you need to leave early, what will happen with the car(s). Is it worth buying through a dealer who would take it back?
☐	8.5.5 Allowance for US cars	How much and for how many and what happens if Earner wants to spend more or less than the allowance?
☐	8.5.6 Tax liabilities	What are the tax liabilities for Earner and over what period of time for a car loan or allowance?
☐	8.5.7 Rental vs. purchase	Is there an allowance to be able to rent long term rather than purchase?
☐	8.5.8 Rental before purchase	How long will you need to rent before you can purchase, and what is in the allowance?
☐	8.5.9 Loan	Is a loan required to help purchase outright? What are the terms and tax liabilities?
☐	8.5.10 More creative solutions	Could you buy a car for a US national and they loan it to you?

8.6 Kids and education

If you think education is expensive, try ignorance.
Derek Bok, former president of Harvard University

Schooling is a huge subject and best discussed in person. But here are the key points.

All schools are divided in the same way, each grade is named the same, and the appropriate grade is based on the child's age on 1st September:

- pre-school age 2½ - 6
- elementary age 6 - 11
- middle 11 - 14
- high 14 - 18

At secondary school level (high school, in particular), the system is very different from the UK in terms of the way the curriculum and lessons are structured. But that doesn't mean your kids won't transfer and adapt easily. We feel it's a far more sensible approach. Instead of studying a 2-year GCSE/A-level syllabus, they study a subject for 1 term and are examined at the end before they're able to move on. One subject builds on the previous, but the students are examined on only one term's worth of information at a time.

America's can-do attitude pervades the school system. If your kids excel in something (sports, math, music…) then an American school can be a really good place for them. The other kids celebrate success and difference. There's no "tall poppy syndrome" here. It's really refreshing.

Public schools

In a given area, there are typically 10 elementary schools, which funnel into 3-4 middle schools, which funnel into 1 high school. Therefore, in one year-group, a high school is likely to have between 700-1000 students. And the Bay Area's numbers are low compared with schools in other parts of the country. Many public schools in the Bay Area have good sports programs and drama facilities.

Public schools are obliged to offer you a place if you live in their catchment area. If you move into the area after the places have been allocated (e.g. part way through the year), your elementary school-age children will be given places at any one of the schools in the area, and not necessarily the closest one. Younger children joining the school later on will be given a place at the nearest school, regardless of where the older siblings are. There are fewer middle schools per area, and even fewer high schools, so children of those ages are more likely to be allocated places in schools close to you.

The public high schools in Marin are the top in the country (and have a much better reputation than the high schools in San Francisco).

Private schools

If you want your children to go to private school, the deadline for applications is the end of January (for Sept start), but most schools extend that deadline for international applicants. However, offers go out mid-March, so if you apply after that time, all the places for that year group will have been allocated. Most private high schools have just under 100 students per year. Private elementary and middle schools have many, many fewer children, and sometimes as few as 20-30 per year.

Fees are $30k (elementary/middle) - $45k (high school) per year, paid up front or in instalments. This figure doesn't cover all the school's costs, though, so there are active fund-raising events throughout the year. The reason for charging less than needed is that the top-up amount you pay can vary according to your ability to pay, and it's tax-deductible. Most schools need an average of $2000-2500 extra, per student, to cover costs. Wealthier families pay a larger top-up than poorer ones, and you decide your own level of contribution.

Every private school in the Bay Area offers financial aid to approximately 30% of their students.

Parochial

Parochial high schools are subsided by religious organizations (usually Catholic or Jewish), so the fees are $15-23k per year – half the cost of secular private schools. They usually have 200-400 students per year group. Their sports facilities are generally better than private schools, but not as good as the public schools.

College and University

If you have university-aged offspring who want to go to college in America, you'll have to go through the process as if that student were applying from Britain. They're over 18 and will have their own visa issues. They'll probably be able to get student visas, but that will be between them and the university they apply to. Most universities love foreign students because they can charge more!

Moving Your Life: BC > Kids and education

☒	Question	Why this matters
☐	8.6.1 International or America	Are you staying in the international system or moving to the American system? If you stay in the international system many, but not all, the questions are irrelevant
☐	8.6.2 Public, private or parochial	This is a question of money, class size, education style and facilities.
☐	8.6.3 UK boarding schools	Depending on where your kids are in the exam cycle, it may easier to send your kids to UK boarding schools to they finish the UK system, and fly them out at vacations.
☐	8.6.4 Financial aid	Most schools offer financial assistance, but is this available based on your visa status?
☐	8.6.5 Location	What is the catchment area for the public school? All schools run the classic yellow school buses, but do they cover your area and where are the pick-up and drop-off points?
☐	8.6.6 Transferring to US system	How old are you kids? There are certain age / school grades when transferring between systems is easier. Transferring mid-term is often not a problem.
☐	8.6.7 Back to UK system	It's far more difficult to get back into the UK system as the kids get older. This may be a factor in how long you plan for the secondment.
☐	8.6.8 Back to UK for university	It's possible to graduate from US high school and apply to either a UK or US university.
☐	8.6.9 Timing of application process	The private and parochial schools have a very set application process milestones. Once they have allocated spaces then it's difficult to get a place.

Moving Your Life: BC > Kids and education

☒	Question	Why this matters
☐	8.6.10 Assessing the schools	Do you need to visit the schools in person, or can you assess them over the phone? Do you need to talk to school's parents to evaluate the schools and how you get the contact details?
☐	8.6.11 Evaluation and entrance exams	The evaluation exams for schools may be quite alien for kids in the UK system: ISEE, SSAT, SAT. Many of the questions you won't even understand, as they're very US culture-specific. How will you apply?
☐	8.6.12 Selecting schools and visits	How you will you decide which schools to short list and final selection? Do you need to visit the short list of schools before making your decision?
☐	8.6.13 Year ahead in UK system	Your kids don't need to go into their correct year group based on their age. But bear in mind that they will be ahead in some areas of a subject such as maths and behind in other areas.
☐	8.6.14 Excel at something	If your kids excel at sports, math, science, drama, music then this may affect your choice of schools. There are schools that specialize in certain subjects and activities.
☐	8.6.15 Practicing religious	The parochial schools are religious, but how much "evidence" do you need to provide before and in the US?
☐	8.6.16 How dominant is religious education	If you're not strongly religious, then how much religious education is part of the school day at the parochial schools?
☐	8.6.17 Leaving early	School fees are annually up-front, but you can buy insurance to cover leaving mid-year.

8.7 How to survive 2 months in "limbo"

Once your belongings get packed into the container, you're on your way – at least emotionally if not physically. When the container arrives in Silicon Valley, you arrive too. But between those two dates there will be two months (plus or minus a few weeks) when you won't have all your belongings. You can choose to stay in the UK for those two months, start your new lives in California, go on an extended world trip or any combination of the above.

But for those 2 months you will have to live with whatever you can beg, borrow and pack in the bags you're taking on the flight with you, ship or leave behind with family and friends.

A lot of this may be decided based on the timing of the move. Perhaps the kids need to be in school for the start of term plus a little time to acclimate (acclimatise). Perhaps the company can't afford to have the Earner take that much vacation.

Staying in a hotel sounds great, but the novelty wears off quickly and 2 months is a long time. There are hotel suites which are like basic mini apartments, but an alternative may be a short term furnished let and AirBnB makes it easier a find a great and affordable property.

Moving Your Life: BC > How to survive 2 months in "limbo"

☒	Question	Why this matters
☐	8.7.1 What is the split of the 2 months	Where will you spend the 2 months? What are the drivers? Can you afford to take time off? Does the Earner need to be in the US earlier than the Supporter?
☐	8.7.2 How do you feel about camping?	What level of compromise and discomfort can you endure? "Camping" at home will seem worse as you expect to have everything you need around you.
☐	8.7.3 Do you have obvious place to stay?	Do you have a holiday home? Does the company have an apartment? Where do you need to be?
☐	8.7.4 Time off	Can you or the business afford to take time off? Is this your chance of a mini-sabbatical?
☐	8.7.5 Do you really use / need that?	Is now the time to really clear out your life? What do you really need to take with you? Have you used/worn it in the last 6 months?
☐	8.7.6 Options	You have multiple options for what you keep for the 2 months. Borrow, rent, buy and donate as you leave, take as luggage on plane, or ship ahead.
☐	8.7.7 What "special" events do you need stuff for?	What "special" things do you need? Will you go skiing, attend black tie parties or wedding, go travelling etc. Do any of these need things you can't rent?
☐	8.7.8 Multiple people	If you have multiple people going to the US are there conflicting timings? Staggering the entry into the US may solve logistical issues around cars, accommodation and "camping".

8.8 Pets

Don't underestimate the difficulty of relocating your pets. They're significant family members. Don't under-estimate the time it takes to research and organize the move and then the cost.

For us, we would not be going if our son's two Chinese Pond Turtles could not come with us. The paperwork required to allow them to travel was huge. And their travel cost the same as seat on the plane with us. In fact, they were in the same plane in Hold 5. But the biggest issue was the time it took trying to find out what had to be done to allow them to travel.

Clearly cats and dogs are way easier. And there are companies that specialize in all kinds of pets such as *www.airpets.com*

Moving Your Life: BC > Pets

☒	Question	Why this matters
☐	8.8.1 How long are you going for?	Are pets joining you or is it easier, based on the time that they would spend in quarantine, for them to stay with family/friends?
☐	8.8.2 Quarantine restrictions?	Can they even be imported, and if so, how long do they spend in quarantine? How will they adapt to it?
☐	8.8.3 What paperwork needed?	Make sure any paperwork is put aside and not packed into the container.
☐	8.8.4 How long do you need before they travel?	Are there certain things that need to be done in advance of travel e.g. health check and monitoring for x months before travel?
☐	8.8.5 Are there 3rd party shippers	Who can make this easier for you?
☐	8.8.6 When do they travel	If they travel at a different time, what happens when they're away from you? Could they travel ahead and spend the 2 months limbo period in quarantine?
☐	8.8.7 Their belongings in a container	Are there things that need to be shipped that can't be in the container (baskets, cages, tanks). If so, what do you do?
☐	8.8.8 Moving back	Once they have gone, can they come back. What restrictions? Do they have to stay in the US a minimum amount of time?

8.9 What does your Supporter do?

What is the Supporter going to do when they get to the US? You can start planning that now. Do they need to start getting some qualifications that will be cheaper and easier to get in the UK?

Don't underestimate how long it takes to get to know your new home, new routines, kids' schools and Earner's schedules/needs. It's a full-time job in itself at first.

With the schools finishing mid-afternoon there is less time between drop-off and collection than in the UK. Plus ferrying them to after-school clubs. It seems a full-time job especially when you add in the volunteer work at school – which is a great way to meet new people.

Think of the secondment as a chance to explore parts of the world which are too far from the UK – Hawaii, Alaska, central and west US, Asia are all within 8 hours flight. Researching and planning these trips to really make the most of the different US vacations (MLK, Presidents, Spring Break, Thanksgiving) takes time.

Moving Your Life: BC > What does your Supporter do?

☒	Question	Why this matters
☐	8.9.1 How long are you going for?	This drives many of the decisions; sabbatical, study or work.
☐	8.9.2 Qualific-ations needed?	Most things are cheaper in the UK, including getting qualifications. But will they be acceptable to the US?
☐	8.9.3 Does the supporter's visa allow paid work?	Not all visas allow the Supporter to work. Do they allow the Supporter to study – and at what cost?
☐	8.9.4 SSN vs. tax ID (W7)?	Not all visas give the Supporter a Social Security Number. Instead they may need to apply for a Tax ID.
☐	8.9.5 Non-work opportunities?	Volunteering, studying, "travel agent", new ventures, reinvention. This is a chance for a new start.
☐	8.9.6 School commitments	Don't overestimate the time you will have available if you have kids to ferry around.
☐	8.9.7 Volun-teering	Can you do voluntary work? All the schools are grateful for time given by parents for various activities ranging from lice checks to organizing fund-raisers.

8.10 Finance

With fluctuating exchange rates, it seems like you always have money in the wrong country. Do you need to bring money from the UK and convert to dollars to buy things; cars, electrical items.

Is the Earner paid in sterling or US dollars? And what currency are credit cards paid in as it will get hit hard in the first few months of set up.

Only 2 credit cards issuers currently recognize your credit rating in the UK when you get to the US and will give you a US credit card from day 1: HSBC Bank and American Express. Every other bank makes you start at zero. So, you pay cash – normally by cheque – for everything.

It has been said before, but it's brutally expensive living here; accommodation, food, services. In fact, anything which has any personal service is scary; music lessons, cleaner, home repairs, babysitting, dog walking, eating out…. The only things that seem cheaper are consumer goods and fuel.

The US tax return can ONLY be filled out by a qualified CPA. It's 70+ pages of unintelligible numbers and questions. Needless to say, the CPA fees are not low, but you don't want to get on the wrong side of the IRS.

Lots of things will be easier if you have thought about them and put things in place when you're in the UK. i.e. getting Amex card, setting up internet banking, signing Power of Attorney forms etc.

You may think that this can be delayed to AC, but there may be things that are required that were put in the container. Doh!!! Better to plan early.

Moving Your Life: BC > Finance

☒	Question	Why this matters
☐	8.10.1 Tax planning in case situation changes	What happens if your company is sold while away? What about a funding round which sets a valuation or triggers options? What happens to visas and what are the tax liabilities?
☐	8.10.2 Timing of move vs. tax year	The US tax year starts 1st Jan. You may be subject to double tax plus the cost of completing tax returns.
☐	8.10.3 Do you have US credit rating?	Without a credit rating then leasing services (e.g. cell phone, home internet) is hard. So, you end up with more expensive options. Think about how you get a credit rating before you arrive.
☐	8.10.4 Where is Earner paid	US or UK. Both to take advantage of tax? And in what currency? How does that change as the exchange rate changes?
☐	8.10.5 Where are expenses paid	Are costs in US Dollars, but paid in Sterling? Is there an agreed exchange rate?
☐	8.10.6 Credit cards	In the early days or weeks of arriving in the US your personal credit card will take a pounding. Is there a high enough credit limit? Paying in US with UK credit cards means you will be nailed on exchange rates. How do you get a US card, or a corporate card?
☐	8.10.7 Forex dealer and slick process	You will need to be able to transfer money easily at a decent rate with as little friction as possible and low fees.
☐	8.10.8 US bank account	Setting up a bank account requires a ton of stuff due to anti-money laundering checks. Can you leverage UK contacts? Do you need to change UK bank to make it easier?
☐	8.10.9 Loans and tax liabilities	Take US tax advice so you avoid double taxation. Some things will be difficult to unpick once you have an official arrival date in the US.

Moving Your Life: BC > Finance

☒	Question	Why this matters
☐	8.10.10 Where are bulk of costs?	US or UK. Can you align the income with those costs?
☐	8.10.11 Investments and pensions	Are your investments structured correctly? If they earn an income that is reinvested, they may be subject to US tax, even though you don't see the income.
☐	8.10.12 Managing UK finances remotely	Do everything you need to whilst you're in the UK and can talk to people, physically sign forms, and show ID, receive cards and security dongles – new accounts, online banking, signatories, power of attorney etc.
☐	8.10.13 Inheritance and gifts	Are there things that need to be in place (e.g. power of attorney, signatories) that are more easily done in the UK?
☐	8.10.14 Critical documents	Any critical documents need to be scanned and originals carried out in hand luggage in case your baggage or container are lost, or where the documents could be required in the 2-month limbo period?

8.11 What gets shipped in the container?

The obvious answer is "everything". But what do you really need to take? Is this a chance to declutter your life, wardrobes and garage? Just because you need it in the UK, will you need it on the West Coast? Remember, your life could be very different here.

But also, there may be things that are best purchased in the UK and they can be shipped at no additional cost as the container is going anyway.

What needs to be kept out of the container because it's needed in the 2-month limbo period?

Assume the container may be lost at sea. What can you not afford to lose – photos, documents, hard disks with photos, music, films? What can be scanned and saved in the cloud?

Don't assume that anything that runs on 240v (and not110v) needs to be sold or thrown away. My very expensive, but old, Bose hifi was 240v only. But a $25 240/110 v transformer fixed that problem.

And finally, some things can't be shipped; liquids… the drinks cabinet.

Moving Your Life: BC > What gets shipped in the container?

☒	Question	Why this matters
☐	8.11.1 What do you really need?	Take are really hard look at everything. What criteria are you going to apply? And to what? Clothes, toys, pictures, ornaments/souvenirs, kitchen stuff.
☐	8.11.2 Radical approach – travel ultra-light	Perhaps this is a chance to travel really, really light and take very little with you. That gives you flexibility in where you stay and would enable you to move around with 6-month leases.
☐	8.11.3 What do you actually use?	Start making a mental note of what gets used.
☐	8.11.4 What will you use?	Try and get a picture of your new life. What will you use? Will you really be giving grand dinner parties? Do you need the silver and crystal, or could they could be put in storage?
☐	8.11.5 What do you need to buy?	High power 240v electrical goods will not work here; hairdryer, toaster, iron. Nor will TVs which are on a different system – but they can be used as big computer monitors with streamed films/TV. What about things with union jacks on – flag, mugs, pictures.
☐	8.11.6 When are you going to do a "declutter" session?	It will take time, be painful and a potential source of conflict; being told you have to toss your favourite 15-year-old fleece (which you never wear). Is this a chance to revamp your wardrobe or update your home style?
☐	8.11.7 Who decides what goes/stays?	What are the criteria? Agree them up front before you start going through each other's stuff and the emotions kick in.
☐	8.11.8 If it doesn't go in the container?	Then what – sold, donated, stored? Selling is time consuming and ultimately makes very little money. Donating to family and then charities is easiest.

Moving Your Life: BC > What gets shipped in the container?

☒	Question	Why this matters
☐	8.11.9 What is needed in 2-month period?	Documents and certificates, warranties, clothes including black tie, technology, specialist toys i.e. ski boots, information for tax returns.
☐	8.11.10 What is too valuable to lose?	Assume the container will get lost at sea. What documents are critical to have the originals? What photos are so sentimentally valuable? Backup drives of music, documents, photos and movies.

Chapter 9

Moving Your Life: AC

We are young, we are one

Let us shine for what it's worth

To your place, place, place

We're on our way, way, way

Lyrics from "We are on our way" by The Royal Concept

ONCE the container is packed and, on its way, then you have essentially moved. You're on our way and it's very exciting. But the work is not over yet. There are a number of things that didn't need to be done Before Container (BC) which now need to be attended to. They could have been done BC, but you were too busy.

Song: We are on our way by The Royal Concept
https://www.youtube.com/watch?v=1ozqJfsepQI

9.1 Packing the container

There is preparation. What are you allowed to take? What should you take? What level of insurance? What packing date?

Then it's the big day. Have you got enough tea, milk and chocolate biscuits for the removals team who will come in and blitz your home?

Are you really ready? You can't be making last minute decisions about what goes or stays as they're packing around you. Better delay the packing if you have not prepared.

Have you taken photos of all valuable items so that if there is an insurance claim at the other end you have evidence of the state they were in before they were packed? Inevitably things will get damaged (or lost/stolen by packers). And you can guarantee the insurance company will try and avoid paying out.

This could be an emotional day as you're essentially "on your way".

Moving Your Life: AC > Packing the container

☒	Question	Why this matters
☐	9.1.1 Planning and estimating	What are you allowed to take? The shippers will come and estimate how much space you need. What else are you going to buy in UK and take e.g. garden furniture, bikes?
☐	9.1.2 What can you not take	Check carefully what can't be taken. Plan what you will do with them – store, sell, donate, dump.
☐	9.1.3 Specialist items	Pianos, wine collections, vehicles all need special attention. Is your shipper capable, and has proven experience of handling them or do you need a specialist shipper? It's more than just putting in a box, but getting through customs in the US.
☐	9.1.4 What level of insurance	Insurance is very expensive. What is your strategy for deciding what level of cover?
☐	9.1.5 The BIG day	You need to be ready and stand well clear. They will arrive with a team who are very efficient at wrapping and packing in large cardboard boxes (packing cases).
☐	9.1.6 Do you know where it's going	Can you mark the boxes based on their location in your new? This will make it easier in the first few weeks when you're trying to open the 3-4 key boxes, out of the 100-150 that are stacked up. Plus, the US shipping team will carry them up or down to the correct rooms. Remember many of the houses around the Bay are on steep hills arranged over multiple floors. If you're initially in temporary accommodation what are the boxes you must have?

Moving Your Life: AC > Packing the container

☒	Question	Why this matters
☐	9.1.7 Is everything going to be unpacked	Are some boxes going into storage at this end or the other end? If they are, do you know what going in the box and did you watch the shippers actually put those items in there? It's better to separate them out so there are no mistakes.[1]
☐	9.1.8 Every-thing not being packed separated	Have you clearly marked and separated anything that is not being packed? If not, it may disappear into a box. There are some real horror stories.[2]
☐	9.1.9 Lists / photos of valuables for insurance	Have you got photo and documented evidence of all critical items? Does it match the level of insurance cover you have paid for?
☐	9.1.10 Camera on hand for breakages	If they break things when packing or dismantling furniture, then be on hand to take photos.
☐	9.1.11 Dismantling / reassembling	Do you need to take photos/ video as they take furniture apart so you can reassemble at the other end?
☐	9.1.12 What happens when container leaves	Empty house.... nearly. Have they packed everything? Are there hidden cupboards they have forgotten?
☐	9.1.13 Packing list	The list of what is in every box, which the shippers get you to sign and give you a copy is a CRITICALLY important set of documents. You will need it in about 2 months time for unpacking. So where are you going to put it?

---

[1] We thought we lost a toolkit. But it was packed in a box with old photographs!!

[2] The worst we heard was the compost box complete with rotting vegetation. For us, they wrapped every item of food in the larder (rice, half eaten tortilla, flour) individually. And also they packed some bottles of wine that were mistakenly mis-delivered to the house on the day of the packing.

9.2 Cars

How are you going to get rid of your UK cars? Selling cars is rarely going to be an easy and uplifting experience. You will lose money. But not nearly as much as selling at short notice – the distressed sale. If you want to understand the bottom price go and get an estimate from www.webuyanycar.com but assume that you will get knocked another £500-1000 based on things they find!!

So, do you need to sell your car? Do you need to use it when you come back to visit the UK? Can you lend it to a friend or relative? If you do this, what is the "contract"? What level of maintenance do they need to give it? What happens if there is a major mechanical problem or they crash it? Or worse they write it off in an accident? What happens if you don't come back?

My pride and joy was a 1999 Lotus Elise which I had owned from new. It was old but I knew its history. I lent it to a friend who was a petrol-head. He loved it and looked after it. When we returned unexpectedly early - 7 months, not 3 years – I got it back. If I had sold it and bought a replacement when I got back, I would have lost thousands of pounds.

Whatever you do, it will cost you more money than simply staying in the UK and owning a car.

Moving Your Life: AC > Cars

☒	Question	Why this matters
☐	9.2.1 What is strategy / commitment?	If you're coming back could you lend vs. sell and buy? Do you need a car for return UK trips? Could you donate to family? There are more options than simply selling.
☐	9.2.2 Best time to sell	Never. But some better than others.
☐	9.2.3 Docs to sell - V5	Make sure the V5 documents to be able to sell it are NOT in the container.[3]
☐	9.2.4 Ship to US	Californian emissions laws are very strict. Unless it's so specialist then this is not a sensible option.
☐	9.2.5 2-month limbo	What are you going to do? Sell or donate at the very end, i.e. just before you leave – the easiest option. Sell to www.webauyanycar.com at the end and accept a low price. Sell at the right time and then rent.
☐	9.2.6 Getting to airport	How are you going to get you and all the bags to the airport? It will probably be more than a normal sized taxi.

---

[3] We didn't do that, but a close friend did. Doh!!!

9.3 Getting rid of stuff you're not taking; donate, dump or drink

Donate, dump, or drink. Or sell but don't expect to get much.

Now the container is left you're committed. Everything that is left needs to go before you do.

You're busy enough, so do you really want the hassle of photographing, posting, selling, packing and shipping something that makes you £8.27?

How about a family car boot sale – offering things to the family first? Donate what's left. And anything charities don't take you will need to take to the dump.

Finally, to get rid of the alcohol you have a "Please DON'T bring a bottle" leaving party.

Moving Your Life: AC > Getting rid of stuff you're not taking; donate, dump or drink

☒	Question	Why this matters
☐	9.3.1 How to decide	You decided before the container left. Now you need to get rid of it. Sell, donate, dump?
☐	9.3.2 Store	You could store things for when you come back. But I am betting that you will never remember you have them, need them or want them. So, you have simply paid for several year's storage for nothing.
☐	9.3.3 Selling	Selling stuff seems a great idea but takes time. The closer you get to your leaving date, the more you have to do. Getting money for things seems to drop in priority.
☐	9.3.4 Family donating	How about a virtual car boot sale to the family? Photographs stuff and send an email to the family on a first come first served basis.
☐	9.3.5 Donation	Not everything can be donated to charity shops. It's worth checking before you load it all into the car.
☐	9.3.6 Dump	You're probably already a regular as you have cleared out the loft and garage.
☐	9.3.7 Alcohol	Party – DO NOT BRING A BOTTLE. Inevitably you will have some left. Do you donate it to the last people leaving the party, or for family?

9.4 Medical, dental, optician

Getting hold of up to date medical, dental and optician records is not a trivial task. But you may need them for medical insurance and to be able to continue any treatments.

You will definitely need your full medical history – including all vaccinations - if you decided to stay and apply for a Green Card.

Is there anything that you need done in the UK on the NHS or through your company medical scheme? It's significantly cheaper in the UK; dental work, a quick hip replacement or new glasses.

Moving Your Life: AC > Medical, dental, optician

☒	Question	Why this matters
☐	9.4.1 Medical records	What medical record do you need? It takes some time to assemble them especially if you have moved around the UK a lot. But is way easier doing it whilst you're still in the UK. Do you have detailed records of any procedures? If not, can you recreate them?
☐	9.4.2 Medical procedures	It's far cheaper to have medical procedures done in the UK privately than in the US – even with US medical insurance.
☐	9.4.3 Medical check up	Is now the time to have a medical check-up on your current medical scheme? For free.
☐	9.4.4 Dental work	It's cheaper to get any dental work done in the UK, but they're not as advanced as the US when it comes to orthodontics (braces).
☐	9.4.5 Glasses or contact lenses	Is it worth getting an eye test and a copy of your prescription? To get contact lenses in the US online you will need a signed prescription from your UK optician.
☐	9.4.6 Vaccination evidence	Schools need evidence of vaccinations for kids.
☐	9.4.7 Alternative therapy	Some approaches e.g. acupuncture, are considered mainstream in the US. Do you need a record of the sessions, diagnosis and approach taken to provide for your US practitioner? Can your UK practitioner explain the specific version that they practice so that you can find exactly the same type of therapist?

9.5 Cancelling stuff and new addresses

The last thing you want to be doing is paying for that travel insurance, magazine subscription of health club in the UK when you're in the US.

Not all are Standing Orders. Some may annual renewals on credit cards that you no longer use, but you have forgotten about.

A quick scan of a year of bank statements and credit card statements should pick up everything. Simply cancelling the credit card will not necessarily kill the subscription renewal. Some credit card accounts are automatically restarted when a subscription hits them. But because the credit card has been cancelled you have no way to pay it!! [4]

---

[4] I kid you not. And as I no longer had a UK address or UK phone number the bank struggled confirm who I was. So they wouldn't let me pay it off as it was considered fraudulent.

☒	Question	Why this matters
☐	9.5.1 Services	Phone, mobile, TV, call monitoring, alarm..
☐	9.5.2 Mobile	Do you want to keep your mobile going in the UK? How will you access messages? How do change the voicemail message from abroad?
☐	9.5.3 Magazines and online	What happens to the unused subscription? They won't deliver to the US, but you will have mail redirection running for a while.
☐	9.5.4 Clubs and associations (sports, business)	If there is a large joining fee can you revert to a low cost Overseas Member or on-hold status? Are there valuable reciprocal memberships?
☐	9.5.5 Insurances	Travel, property, health all need cancelling. But only once you have arrived in the US. You may be covered by travel and health for a short time after arriving as you're "on vacation".
☐	9.5.6 Investments	Investments can continue whilst you're in the US, but your financial advisor may not be able to offer advice once you are living in the US. Have you set them up for continued payments?
☐	9.5.7 Charitable donations	Do you want to transfer your donations to
☐	9.5.8 Mail redirection	You will need this for at least a year. But where do you get it directed, until you get a permanent US address?
☐	9.5.9 US vs. UK addresses	Not every UK organization can cope with a US address and phone number. For some, you will need a UK address; parent, sibling, close friend. They will need to be able to open mail, scan the important stuff, toss the junk and hold onto it until you pop in to collect it. Therefore, it's probably not an accountant or PO box.

☒	Question	Why this matters
☐	9.5.10 Elderly monitoring	Are you currently one of the people who are alerted if an elderly relative or friend hits a panic button? Who can take over from you?

9.6 Leaving parties

You're leaving and some people you may never see again. Some you will be happy to never see again!! Others you will lose touch with. Those you care about; you will see when you come back or they will take advantage of your trip and visit San Francisco.

There will be parties for friends. There will be parties for the kids – possibly combined with early birthday parties. And finally, there will be the family parties. Plus, the sending off at the airport.

There are also the one to one lunches or dinners with those who you want to see but not in the crush of a party.

Moving Your Life: AC > Leaving parties

☒	Question	Why this matters
☐	9.6.1 Company party	You're not leaving the company, just on secondment and back regularly. So, a company party is probably not appropriate.
☐	9.6.2 Big party for friends	This is where you get rid of the alcohol
☐	9.6.3 Kids parties	Can you combine the kids' friends party with a birthday party?
☐	9.6.4 Family	How many? Are family spread out so you need multiple events, or is this an excuse to get everyone together?
☐	9.6.5 One on ones	Who needs special attention? Granny? Close friend too ill to travel?
☐	9.6.6 Leaving at airport	Keep it to a minimum. It's hard enough as it is for grandparents, parents and kids.
☐	9.6.7 Who to invite to SF	Who will you make a personal invite to visit you? If you offer, then they will probably take you up on it.
☐	9.6.8 Organising parties	Everything you own (plates, cups etc.) are all in the container. Pizza and plastic / paper cups works well.
☐	9.6.9 Where	Can you use your house, or have you already moved out and rented it?

9.7 Flying to the US & arriving in one piece: a long, emotional day

Which flight? It's a long flight and an 8-hour time change so it's tough. An early start means you arrive in SF in daylight – but still tired. A later start means it's easier at the UK end, but very late when you get to SFO. And once you land you need to negotiate immigration. This is probably the first time with your shiny new visa, not an ESTA. So, the process will take longer. So, use the flight to get some sleep rather than watching films for 11 hours straight.

There will be nervousness from the Supporter and kids so meticulous planning is key.

There will be tears at the airport as you leave.

If you're arriving with 2-3 suitcases each, then how are you getting from the airport? Hire car, taxi, being collected, UberSUV? Is one of you getting out early and can meet you at the airport?

If you get a hire car, it will need to be a large SUV, which is expensive. And you will need to drive back to SFO to swap it for the longer-term hire car until you buy a car. Renting a car just adds another hour at the end of a very long day. So, whilst it may seem a good idea when you're booking it in the UK you may regret it when you arrive in SFO.

Pack everything you need for the first night in hand luggage. The last think you need is to have your main baggage get lost or delayed. It just adds to the stress of the day.

For us, we got through immigration, collected the hire car and then had to try and find the turtles. They had arrived on the same flight but were in a customs warehouse somewhere in SFO which involved a paper chase around 3 separate offices. And then a long wait whilst they were collected in their wooden crate. Then it was off to SF where we had rented a house for a month, but the keys needed to be collected from another location first. It was a LONG and emotional day.

It's worth spending a little money to make this an easier day; taxis, food, flights, hotels. Don't be tempted to do public transport, economy flight, public transport, cheap hotel…..

Moving Your Life: AC > Flying to the US & arriving in one piece: a long, emotional day

☒	Question	Why this matters
☐	9.7.1 Which flight?	What time is it best to arrive? What class of flight – economy, premium, business? Pay for a direct flight. It's bad enough without fighting to make connections and the risk of delays.
☐	9.7.2 Luggage allowances	How many bags are you taking? Is it cheaper to ship bags than pay excess baggage charges – and less hassle. Where would you get them shipped to?
☐	9.7.3 Getting to the airport	Who is taking you to the airport? Is it a big send off with tears?
☐	9.7.4 Getting from the airport	How are you getting from SFO? Taxi, hire car, friend?
☐	9.7.5 Where to stay	Where are you staying the first night? Airport hotel? Airbnb house/apartment? Permanent house/apartment? Suite hotel?
☐	9.7.6 Pets	What are the logistics? Be very clear on the instructions and be very clear what documentation you need and where you need to go. Reuniting with your pets comes at the end of a long day.
☐	9.7.7 Hand luggage	What goes in hand luggage, bearing in mind there are only 2 sorts of luggage- "lost luggage and hand luggage".

9.8 Unpacking the container

150 boxes stacked in the garage. Hmm. I wonder what is in all of them? And do we really need it. We lived without it for 2 months.

You will not know when the boxes will arrive. The ship could take anywhere from 4-8 weeks to cross the Atlantic and make it up the Pacific coast. But then US customs can take as short or as long as they need to clear it. They could demand that every box is opened – at your cost.

Ideally, you will get a few days notice that it has cleared customs. Before then it's worth contacting the US shippers so they can assess how easy or difficult it will be to unload at your new home. Many locations are very hilly so getting a 40-foot container right up to the door is difficult. In the north bay the roads are also very narrow with very steep drives. So, it's worth getting the shippers to scope out your house so they arrive with the right team and kit.

This is also where you find out how well the things were packed. Get the camera ready and the packing checklist for any insurance claim items. Check the insurance small print. You will probably need to claim within x months of the packing date. So, don't wait to see if the creases will come out of the sofa or jacket before claiming. Here speaks the voice of experience.

Moving Your Life: AC > Unpacking the container

☒	Question	Why this matters
☐	9.8.1 When	You have no control over the shipping time and Customs. Plan on 8 weeks, but don't rely on it.
☐	9.8.2 Who supervises	You need to plan. Which rooms are boxes going into? It's easier to get the shippers to carry stuff up and downstairs. You will need your copy of the packing sheet from 2 months ago!!
☐	9.8.3 Every-thing unpacked	Do you want everything unpacked? Sounds great but until you decide where all the kitchen stuff goes you cause more problems. However, EVERYTHING should be unpacked in time to make any insurance claim.
☐	9.8.4 Items in storage	Are you going to unpack and repack the items in storage or just get them sent straight to storage? Where are you going to record what you sent?
☐	9.8.5 Furniture reassembled	Get the shippers to assemble furniture. They have done it so many times – without the IKEA manuals!!!
☐	9.8.6 Breakages and loss	Stuff will get broken. Some may have "disappeared". Take photos and get it recorded against the packing list.
☐	9.8.7 Insurance claim	Read the small print. What do you need to do? Get on with it.
☐	9.8.8 Tip for the shippers	The US is a tipping culture. So, you'll need some cash for the guys who will have worked hard.
☐	9.8.9 Packing boxes	Not everything will be unpacked. You will end up with a garage of boxes. Don't throw all the boxes. Stack them flat as they're useful for storage later.

Chapter 10

Other considerations

If the grass is greener on the other side of the fence, you can bet the water bill is higher

Anon

THIS chapter is all the other things that are not directly related to the physical move. Starting with what are your motivations. Is the commitment there from you AND your family. Has the company budgeted enough to be able to make sure you do not have a huge drop in standard of living due to the move, no matter what happens to the exchange rate?

Whilst we are not visa lawyers, we can say with certainty "No visa, no move".

Finally, a few thoughts on fitting in.

10.1 Why bother?

So, you need to be clear what the driver is for coming to the US.

I have no idea what Columbus' business case was for sailing across the Atlantic, but I am sure it wasn't "Sounds like a bit of fun and it will be easier than staying at home". Various reports suggest his objective was to sail west until he reached Asia (the Indies) where he would find gold, pearls and spice. Your objective – and that of the Gold Rush pioneers – is probably similar.

The 49er Gold Rush motivated 300,000 people to travel to California in the 1800s, enduring hardship and risking death. At first, most Argonauts (as they were also known) travelled by sea. From the East Coast, a sailing voyage around the tip of South America would take five to eight months and cover some 18,000 nautical miles. An alternative was to sail to the Atlantic side of the Isthmus of Panama and walk with canoes and mules for a week through the jungle. Once on the Pacific side, the pioneers would wait for a ship sailing for San Francisco. There was a third route across Mexico starting at Veracruz. And many gold-seekers took the overland route across the vast continental stretch of the United States, particularly along the California Trail. Each of these routes had its own deadly hazards, from shipwreck to typhoid fever, from cholera to snow-bound cannibalism.

Gold and riches await you in Silicon Valley too. Now getting here is easier. There are regular flights every day into San Francisco. But once you get here the business landscape can still be very unforgiving. It will take a pioneering spirit and plenty of resolve.

Do you have what it takes?

Other considerations > Why bother?

☒	Question	Why this matters
☐	10.1.1 What commitment level?	See Chapter 3: Go big or go home
☐	10.1.2 What will make you retrench?	It's worth planning for the divorce, not the honeymoon. Pulling out of the US with your tail between your legs is painful psychologically, financially and sets the company back. It's worth thinking about what failure looks like and discussing it openly.
☐	10.1.3 Company politics?	Will company politics get in the way of being successful? If senior execs are in the US, how will that change the balance of power, and potential encourage fiefdoms and politics back at home?
☐	10.1.4 Too much change?	This is another huge change project. Has the company already got a number of competing change projects underway (product, markets, staffing) that mean the company does not have the capacity to execute on the US expansion?
☐	10.1.5 Existing US team	Do you already have existing US staff? How will this change their responsibilities and the relationships with the UK?
☐	10.1.6 First attempt	Is this the first time you have established a team in the US? If not, are there preconceptions, politics or organizational structures that need to be broken down?

Other considerations > Is there enough budget allocated?

10.2 Is there enough budget allocated?

It is brutally expensive to live here, so has the company allocated enough budget for you to do your job with a decent standard of living for you and the family.

Other considerations > Is there enough budget allocated?

☒	Question	Why this matters
☐	10.2.1 Banking	Who are you going to bank with? Remember not all banks are in all US states, even the ones that claim to be global.
☐	10.2.2 Credit rating	You will have no credit rating when you get to the US. Everything is cash up front.
☐	10.2.3 Renting office space	Where is the office? Office space is at a premium in certain "cool" areas of Silicon Valley and the City. Do you REALLY need to be in the cool area? Can you sub-let from a partner or another start-up that has over capacity whilst they grow?
☐	10.2.4 Payroll	Has the company set up US payroll and budgeted for the US payroll taxes?
☐	10.2.5 Medical benefits	Have you budgeted medical benefits? More importantly, have you understood the thousand different options and the related costs? The costs to employees for medical expenses can be significant even if they have insurance cover, but the wrong level – i.e. the cheapest policies have a deductible (excess) of $12,000 per year. And the costs of all medical are huge – a trip to A&E could easily be $1,500; an overnight in hospital $20,000.
☐	10.2.6 Exchange rates	The US exchange rates are fluctuating wildly, so the cost of living in the US could get very expensive or seem cheap. Have you budgeted conservatively?
☐	10.2.7 Paying secondment costs	How are you paying the secondment costs? Is it via staff expenses? Is it from a US located US dollar account? Is it from a UK US dollar account? Do you have a company US dollar credit card?

Other considerations > Is there enough budget allocated?

☒	Question	Why this matters
☐	10.2.8 Look-see visits	These are not cheap, and it feels like you have been sent with you family on an all-expenses paid vacation. It won't feel like that so don't let the company make you foot some of the costs.
☐	10.2.9 Relocation packages & contract	This is a LONG list. The contract needs to accommodate all eventualities.
☐	10.2.10 Tax implications	Have you considered all the tax implications; corporate UK, corporate US, personal taxes in both UK and US? Who is paying the additional tax burden?
☐	10.2.11 Trans-atlantic trips: business	How often do you need to fly back for UK meetings? What happens if you want to bring families back?
☐	10.2.12 Trans-atlantic trips: visiting family	How often are you budgeting that the you will come back to the UK? What about flying families back?
☐	10.2.13 End of secondment	At the end of the secondment you have all the moving fees, but also the costs of winding up leases and rentals. When is this planned? Is this budgeted for?
☐	10.2.14 Early return	What happens if you decide, or are forced to come back early? This may be impossible to include in a total budget, but it's worth thinking about to set budgets or allowances.
☐	10.2.15 Tax	US federal and California tax and filing dues. Who pays additional tax for you if they're out of pocket due to the move?

10.3 Visas

First, let's make one thing very clear. No visa = no secondment.

You can have staff travelling back and forth on a visitor visa (ESTA), but this is not a long-term solution for a number of reasons. Eventually US Immigration will pick up on the frequent entries and make it difficult for your staff; the flying and jetlag due to an 8-hour time change burns people out; and until staff are firmly established in the US they won't be taken seriously.

So, it all starts with getting visas for the people who are transferring to the US.

There are a number of different visa options. Take a look at the case studies at the end of the book to see the wide range of visas acquired.

It's not our place to try and offer advice. It's a legal minefield and you need specific, targeted help. Getting it wrong costs money and time. You need a visa lawyer.

The questions here help you think about what your visa needs to cover.

Other considerations > Visas

☒	Question	Why this matters
☐	10.3.1 What type of visa	There are a range of visa types, each with their own specific rules and allocations, which vary from year to year.
☐	10.3.2 Visa lawyers	Who are you using – a US lawyer or a US located in UK?
☐	10.3.3 Timing	When do you need the visa? Is it tied to time working for the company?
☐	10.3.4 Plan B	If you can't get visas is there an alternative; another visa type or commuting?
☐	10.3.5 Supporter and kids	What does the visa allow your supporter to do; work, student, health insurance? What about kids and s / college?
☐	10.3.6 Green Card	Can you easily apply for a Green Card, and when?
☐	10.3.7 Significant event	What happens if the company is acquired or closes down its US operation?
☐	10.3.8 Costs	What are the complete costs, including premium processing if required?
☐	10.3.9 Renewal	What happens when the end of the visa term is reached?
☐	10.3.10 SSN or tax ID	Does the visa get a social security numbers (SSN) for the Earner or the entire family? Without an SSN everything is more difficult; driving license, credit card, bank account, medical insurance.
☐	10.3.11 Passports	Do they need to be renewed? It's FAR easier in the UK than when in the US.

10.4 Fitting into the US culture

You don't have to pretend to be an American, mimic the accent and celebrate July 4th. There is a real value in being British, which you shouldn't lose. However, you do need to make sure that you build a company and culture that works well in the US. It's not the UK and therefore you can't behave and operate as though it were.

Other considerations > Fitting into the US culture

☒	Question	Why this matters
☐	10.4.1 How American	Are you going to convert the image of the whole company to be American or just the US operation?
☐	10.4.2 Dress code	There is a different dress code here. It's important to fit in.
☐	10.4.3 Language	As Mark Twain said, "England and US are 2 countries divided by a common language". It's surprising how many words are different.
☐	10.4.4 Humour	Tread carefully around humour in the workplace.
☐	10.4.5 PC	Tread EVEN more carefully around political correctness, especially in the Bay area, where it seems people go to extreme lengths to make sure that they don't offend.
☐	10.4.6 Networking	There is no lack of opportunities as there are events almost every day of the week on some tech related topic or other in the Bay area. Some paid, some free.
☐	10.4.7 Alcohol	A glass of wine at lunchtime could brand you an alcoholic! The Americans don't drink during the day, even at business lunches.
☐	10.4.8 Britishness	Don't lose your Britishness. It's valuable. Morph it.

Chapter 11

It wasn't like that for me

To acquire knowledge, one must study; but to acquire wisdom, one must observe.

Marilyn vos Savant (author, lecturer, playwright and listed in Guinness Book of Records under "Highest IQ")

IT is going to be different for everyone who relocates because they have a different set of circumstances. So, we have interviewed a number of people who have made the move and asked them to give us their story. But also, we asked them for one thing they wished they'd known or done.

Now life isn't always fun. Some of the stories are painful and expensive. But that makes them all the more valuable.

If we'd interspersed these stories with the questions it would have made the Chapters too long. It would also have prevented you using the questions as checklists or aide-memoires. So, we've grouped together our list of stories in this Chapter. I'm sure that you have your own stories – both positive and negative - so let us know them.

And finally, welcome to Silicon Valley.

It wasn't like that for me

Ian and Natalie

Commitment level

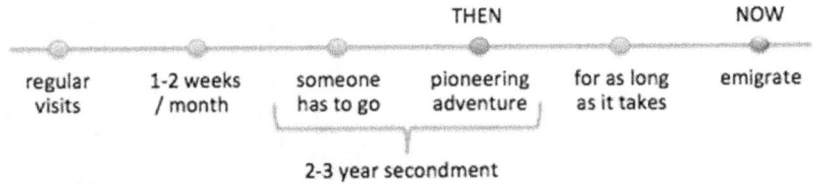

Background

They're married and both have British passports. Ian was CEO of NimbusPartners living in the UK. The entire family moved in 2011 to support growth of NimbusPartners; daughter was 13 and son was 11. NimbusPartners was acquired so after 7 months had to return to the UK within a week of the acquisition due to expiry of visas. They returned to US in 2013 intending to stay long term. Both children are in the US private school system.

Visa

Ian applied and got an E2 in 2011. In 2013 to return to US he managed to get an O1 with the fantastic title of "Individual of Extraordinary Ability". The family now has Green Cards.

What surprised you most?

The cost of living.

Best thing about being here?

The weather which enables you to be doing things outside most of the year, combined with having a stunning house on the water.

What do you wish you'd known / done?

We had some damage from the shipping including creases in the leather sofas. Waited to see if the creases would come out with time, but then missed the 30-day cut off in which to declare an intent to make a claim. The insurers, naturally, used this to refuse all claims, including significant damage to our grand piano. Doh!!!

Adrian and Kim

Commitment level

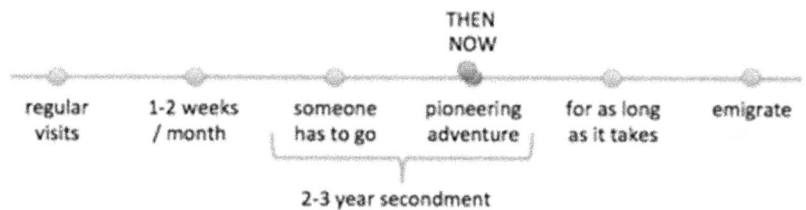

Background

Adrian and Kim are both British Nationals. They have 2 children who were aged 11 and 9 when they moved.

Adrian was COO of NimbusPartners and moved out with Ian to drive the growth of the business and provide confidence to potential US investors that the business was serious about the North American market. NimbusPartners was acquired after only 7 months and visa was no longer valid, so Adrian and family had to return back to the UK.

Visa

Adrian got an E2, but initially had an application for an L1 rejected

What is the best thing about being here?

The 'can do' attitude.

What is the hardest thing?

Dealing with the time zone to ensure that I was connected back home with the office.

What do you wish you'd known / done?

Left all our possessions in the UK and just bought stuff to equip the house out here.

How did you do the 2 months without belongings?

Bought a few things, lived quite rough, prayed that the container would turn up before Christmas.

It wasn't like that for me

Mark and Rusi

Commitment level

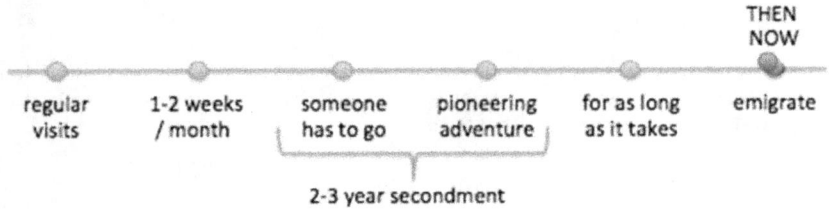

Background

Mark (British) met Rusi over 5 years ago in London. Mark was born and raised in London. Rusi (American) has spent the majority of her life living in the Bay Area and was in London for work. Rusi's employer wanted her to return to San Francisco. Rusi was happy to move back and Mark decided to move with her.

Visa

Mark had a K1 Fiancé Visa. The application was submitted June 2014 and approved November 2014. The visa stipulates that:

- Mark enter the US within 90 days of the November 2014 approval date;
- Mark and Rusi marry within 90 days of Mark's entry date to the US.

Once married, Mark was able to apply for:

- Adjustment of status (i.e. green card)
- Employment authorization document (i.e. work permit)
- Advanced parole (allows Mark to travel outside of the US and re-enter the US while the green card is in process).

Once the employment authorization document has been issued, Mark will work as if he were a US national i.e. not tied to a particular company, skill or profession and doesn't require third-party sponsorship.

It wasn't like that for me

What is the best thing about being here?

Weather. Mark and Rusi enjoy outdoor activities, which the weather allows for. California is known for its sunny climate, but Mark and Rusi also enjoy skiing, which can be enjoyed within a 3.5 hour drive away.

What surprised you most?

Very expensive house prices and traffic congestion. On the latter, people are far more dependent on driving, perhaps because of the culture, but also because public transport is not as widely available compared to London. Mark found it impossible to get around (in San Ramon, East Bay) while he did not have a car. Buses are underserved in residential areas.

Mark was also surprised at the high cost of private medical insurance.

What is the hardest thing?

Waiting for work permit to be issued.

What do you wish you'd known / done?

Mark wishes that he had all of the required vaccinations done before having the visa medical examination in the UK. US immigration requires that visa applicants have a certain list of vaccinations completed, prior to applying for a green card. In the UK, these vaccinations are free. However, Mark had these vaccinations done in the US, which cost over $350. In hindsight, Mark would've visited his GP in the UK prior to the visa medical, in order to have all the vaccinations done.

How did you do the 2 months without belongings?

This wasn't an issue for Mark, given that Rusi was from the Bay Area. Rusi already owned an apartment, which was fully furnished and equipped. Mark left the UK with only two suitcases.

It wasn't like that for me

Jonathan and Alyssa

Commitment level

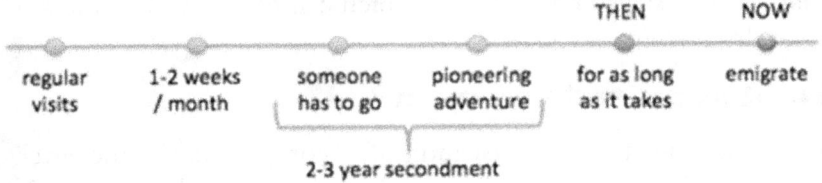

Background

Alyssa is a US citizen and is married to Jonathan, a British citizen. They were both living in the UK and wanted to move to the US. When they moved over Jonathan was CEO of a start-up and Alyssa didn't have a job.

Visa

Alyssa already had a US passport and Jonathan applied for and got his green card in the UK before they moved.

What is the best thing about being here?

Can-do, positive attitude of people

What surprised you most?

How quickly they found like-minded friends

What is the hardest thing?

Leaving 4 kids (2 at boarding school and 2 at college) back in the UK.

What do you wish you'd known / done?

Wish they had known that Jonathan could apply for citizenship after 3 years not 5.

How did you do the 2 months without belongings?

They left the UK a long time before the container as they still had a family home that hadn't been sold. So, they rented a 1-bedroom apartment and bought the little that they needed.

Simon and Jessica

Commitment level

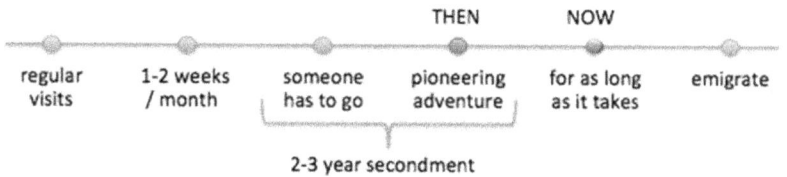

Background & Visa

Simon and Jessica were married with a 15-month-old son. They were used to moving, having lived in the UK and Switzerland. Simon was working in the UK for a quoted US software company with its HQ in San Francisco. The US CEO wanted Simon to work in US HQ but there were no H1B visas available. So, Simon worked in the UK in the new role with 1 week a month trips to US until he had enough time in role to qualify for L1 visa.

Best thing about being here?

Spectacular surroundings and weather.

What surprised you most?

Having moved several times, you just throw yourself into it. But that was when we were a couple. It was different with a 15-month-old and it took longer to get settled this time.

What is the hardest thing?

Being a 12-hour flight away from family and friends.

How did you do the 2 months without belongings?

We had good relocation package, a corporate fully-furnished apartment in San Francisco, and we air freighted several boxes of essentials out.

Biggest regret?

I think if you are the sort of person who is happy to move your entire life to another country, you spend your time looking

It wasn't like that for me

forwards not backwards. So, I am not the sort of person who has regrets.

Chapter 12

The Final Word

A conclusion is the place where you got tired of thinking.
Albert Bloch (American Artist, 1882 – 1961)

WHEN talking to people about moving to the US I think I can summarize it as the most stressful, most expensive and the best thing we have ever done. It has changed our life. And it was worth it.

So, we will give Andre Gide the last word:

Man cannot discover new oceans unless he has the courage to lose sight of the shore.

Notes pages

We hope that this book has inspired you and that you have already scribbled your thoughts all over it. However, if you have ideas that need a little more space then please use these notes pages.

Notes pages

www.ingramcontent.com/pod-product-compliance
Lightning Source LLC
Chambersburg PA
CBHW071513150426
43191CB00009B/1509